Phonetic Bible Stories

The Parable of the Good Samaritan

Luke 10:25–37

W9-BVE-335

The Tan Man

Claudia Courtney ☆ **Illustrated by Larry Nolte**

CPH
SAINT LOUIS

For Lynn, a faithful friend who loves to serve. Ecclesiastes 9:10a

Copyright © 1999 Concordia Publishing House
3558 S. Jefferson Avenue, St. Louis, MO 63118-3968
Manufactured in the United States of America

1 2 3 4 5 6 7 8 9 10   08 07 06 05 04 03 02 01 00 99

Note to Grown-ups

The love of reading is one of the greatest things you can instill in your child. It opens new horizons, exposes your child to new ideas, and provides information as well as entertainment.

This beginning reader series blends the best of two worlds— phonics to help your child learn to read and popular Bible stories to help your child learn to read God's Word. After you use a book in this series, open your child's Bible and read the story from God's Word. Emphasize to your child that this story is not make-believe, it's a parable. Jesus used parables to teach truths about God and His Kingdom.

Before you begin, review together the word, sound, and spelling lists on page 16. This story emphasizes the phoneme that makes the short ă sound as in man.

After your review, read the story to your child, exaggerating the designated phonetic sound or sounds. Discuss the illustrations. Your enthusiasm for reading, and especially for reading God's Word, should be contagious. Run your finger under each word as you read it, showing your child that it is the words that convey the actual story. Have your child join with you in reading repeated phrases.

Finally, have your child read the story as you offer plenty of praise. Pause to allow your youngster time to sound out words, but provide help when necessary to avoid frustration. When a mistake is made, invite your child to reread the sentence. This provides an appropriate opportunity to guide your early reader.

Please remember that your child is learning and blending a complex set of new skills. Early success and your generous praise are keys to opening the door to your child's world of reading, especially to the joys of reading the Bible.

Claudia Courtney

Jesus told this story.

A man traveled the zigzag path.

He had his cash in his pack on his back.
He had his mat and sack in his hands.

A snag!
A band of mad men had a bad plan.
The bandits had a trap to catch the man.

Attack! Grab! Jab! Slap!

The bandits yanked his pack and sack.
They nabbed his cash and his mat and
ran fast.

The bandits left the sad man flat.
He needed help off the path.

A man from the temple traveled
the zigzag path.
He glanced at the sad man and
passed.
He did not help.

Another man traveled the zigzag
path.
He glanced at the sad man and
passed.
He did not help.

At last, a tan man from another
land traveled the zigzag path.
He glanced at the sad man.
He began his good plan to help.

The tan man used rags to
    bandage the sad man.
He put him on his donkey and
    began the path back.

The tan man took the sad man to
    an inn to get well.
He spent his own cash and said
    he would be back to help.

The sad man began to be glad and thanked the tan man.

Jesus said we show our love for God when we do kind acts like the tan man.

Word Lists

phoneme *a*

acts	began	land	ran
an	cash	last	sack
and	catch	mad	sad
another	fast	man	slap
at	flat	mat	snag
attack	glad	nabbed	tan
back	glanced	pack	trap
bad	grab	passed	traveled
band	had	path	zigzag
bandage	hands	plan	
bandits	jab	rags	

Other Words

a	him	of	the
be	his	off	they
did	in	on	this
do	inn	our	to
donkey	Jesus	own	told
for	kind	put	took
from	left	said	used
get	like	show	we
God	love	spent	well
good	men	story	when
he	needed	temple	would
help	not	thanked	yanked